Facts About Countries
Australia

Dana Meachen Rau

FRANKLIN WATTS
LONDON • SYDNEY

First published in 2005 by
Franklin Watts
96 Leonard Street, London
EC2A 4XD

Franklin Watts Australia
Level 17/207 Kent Street
Sydney NSW 2000

Facts About Countries is based on the Country
Files series published by Franklin Watts. It is
produced for Franklin Watts by Bender
Richardson White, PO Box 266, Uxbridge, UK.
Editor: Lionel Bender
Designer and Page Make-up: Ben White
Picture Researcher: Cathy Stastny
Cover Make-up: Mike Pilley, Radius
Production: Kim Richardson

Graphics and Maps: Stefan Chabluk
Educational Advisor: Prue Goodwin, Institute of
Education, The University of Reading
Consultant: Dr Terry Jennings, a former
geography teacher and university lecturer. He is
now a full-time writer of children's geography
and science books.

A CIP catalogue record for this book is available
from the British Library.

ISBN 0-7496-6036-8
Dewey Classification 919.4

Printed in China

Picture Credits

The Author

Dana Meachen Rau is a full-time writer and editor of non-fiction books. She has written more than 10 books for children about countries of the world.

Note to parents and teachers

Every effort has been made by the Publishers to ensure that the websites in this book are suitable for children, that they are of the highest educational value, and that they contain no inappropriate or offensive material. However, because of the nature of the Internet, it is impossible to guarantee that the contents of these sites will not be altered. We strongly advise that Internet access is supervised by a responsible adult.

Contents

Welcome to Australia

Australia is the largest island in the world. It lies between the Indian and South Pacific Oceans in an area of the world called Oceania.

A land of contrast

Australia lies below the equator in the southern hemisphere. This means that its winter is from June to August, and summer from December to February. Australia has large, modern, busy cities along its coast. Its countryside, called 'the Outback', is mostly empty, flat and quiet.

Below. **The centre of the city of Melbourne is filled with modern skyscraper buildings.**

Deserts and forests

The west of Australia is mostly a raised, flat region of very dry deserts. In the centre is Uluru (Ayers Rock), the world's largest single block of rock, 330m (1,100ft) high.

Most rain falls along the coast, where more people live and work than elsewhere in Australia. Rainforests grow in the north and south of the country.

Right. **A red kangaroo.**

Below. **Comparing the summer and winter temperatures in five different cities.**

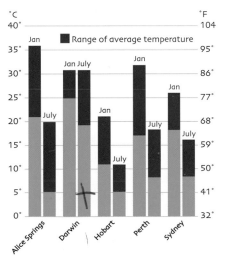

The People

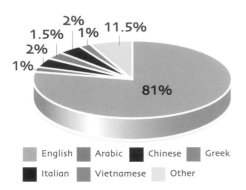

English ■ Arabic ■ Chinese ■ Greek
■ Italian ■ Vietnamese ■ Other

Above. **Most people in Australia speak English, but there are also many native languages.**

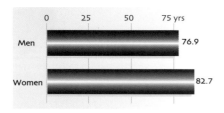

Above. **Age men and women can expect to live to.**

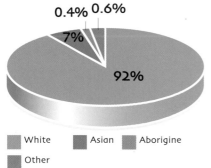

■ White ■ Asian ■ Aborigine
■ Other

Above. **Different races in Australia.**

Right. **An Aboriginal hunter. He is holding traditional weapons, including a spear and a boomerang.**

8

Australians are mostly a mix of native people, the Aborigines, and people whose families came from Europe and Asia in the 1800s and early 1900s.

Ancient ways of life

The Aborigines came to Australia about 40,000 years ago from Asia. They hunted with spears and boomerangs and gathered food from the land. People around the world have learned about Aboriginal history and beliefs from their cave and rock paintings, which are found all over Australia.

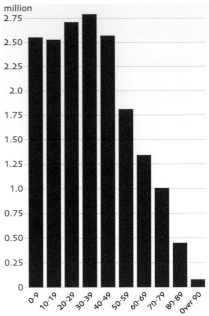

Above. **Numbers of people of different ages in the Australian population.**

Left. **The parents of these children playing at an outdoor party came to Australia from many different countries.**

People from all over the world

British settlers were the first newcomers to Australia, in 1788. They came to farm or raise sheep. In the 1850s, many people from China arrived to work in gold mines.

Since 1945, more than five million people have moved to Australia from over 150 countries. Today, there are less than 800,000 Aborigines. Most of them live in the cities and towns, but a few still live in the Outback in the same way as their ancestors did.

Web Search ▶▶

▶ www.immi.gov.au
Details about immigrants to Australia.

▶ www.atsic.gov.au
www.aiatsis.gov.au
About Aborigines and other Australians.

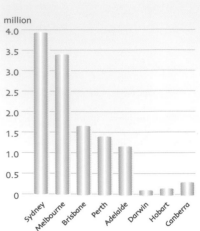

Above. The number of people living in Australia's main cities.

Below. A long, straight road in central Australia. Many roads in the Outback look like this.

Above. This house in the suburbs of Brisbane is built of bricks and wood, with a tiled roof. It is like the houses built by the first British settlers in Australia in the early 1800s

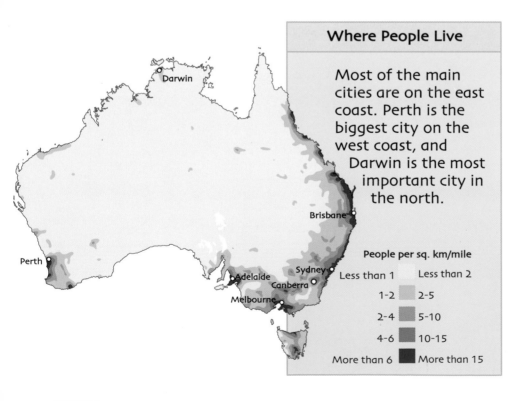

Where People Live

Most of the main cities are on the east coast. Perth is the biggest city on the west coast, and Darwin is the most important city in the north.

People per sq. km/mile

Less than 1	Less than 2
1-2	2-5
2-4	5-10
4-6	10-15
More than 6	More than 15

Town and Country Life

More than 85 per cent of Australians live and work in cities in the south-eastern corner of the country.

Big cities

The capital city of Australia is Canberra, but Sydney has more people. Sydney is the main commercial city and has the biggest port. Melbourne, the second-largest city, is another huge business centre.

Web Search ▶▶

▶ www.cityofsydney.nsw.gov.au
Sydney's official website.

▶ www.act.gov.au/index.jsp
Canberra's official website.

▶ www.flyingdoctor.net
The Royal Flying Doctor Service.

Life in suburbs and countryside

Most people live in single-storey family houses in the suburbs that surround the cities. These houses have gardens and verandas where people can relax in the evening after work.

Life in the countryside is very different. People there are mostly farmers, fruit-growers or miners. Many farms are so large that people need to drive to see their neighbours. They may visit the nearest town for supplies only once a week. Their houses are big, with space for the family to live and work. There are barns for storage.

Farming and Fishing

Two-thirds of Australia is used for farming or grazing. Fishing is carried out along the coast.

Raising animals, growing crops

Most land is used as grazing for cattle and sheep. There are 150 million sheep in Australia. Their wool is the main export. In many parts of the country, it is difficult to grow crops because of flooding and droughts.

Australia produces butter, cheese and yoghurt. Many farmers keep poultry and 90,000 chickens are sold for meat each year. The main crops are sugar-cane, wheat and barley. Farmers also grow rice, oats, cotton, and vegetables such as carrots, potatoes and tomatoes. Australian fruits include oranges, pineapples, grapes and apples.

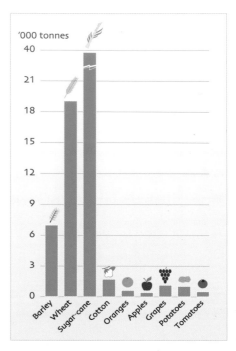

Above. **Quantities of the main crops grown each year.**

Right. **Wheat is harvested from a farm in Western Australia.**

The fishing industry

Offshore fishing boats catch mostly marlin, tuna, prawns, lobsters and oysters. Many of the shellfish are sold to Japan. Oysters, prawns and even crocodiles are raised in fish farms and artificial lakes.

Left. Sheep are sheared once a year. The merino sheep is the most popular type. It produces beautifully soft, fine wool.

Right. Weights of fish and shellfish caught by sea-going boats.

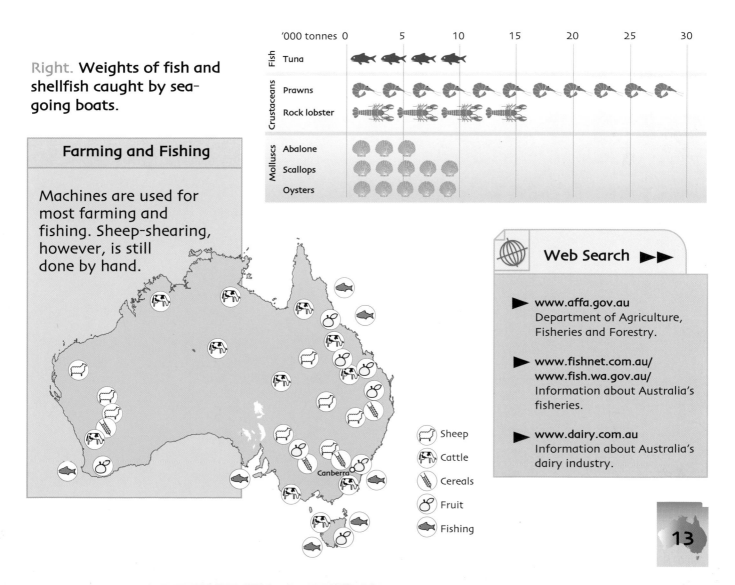

Farming and Fishing

Machines are used for most farming and fishing. Sheep-shearing, however, is still done by hand.

Web Search ▶▶

▶ www.affa.gov.au
Department of Agriculture, Fisheries and Forestry.

▶ www.fishnet.com.au/
www.fish.wa.gov.au/
Information about Australia's fisheries.

▶ www.dairy.com.au
Information about Australia's dairy industry.

Sheep
Cattle
Cereals
Fruit
Fishing

13

Resources and Industry

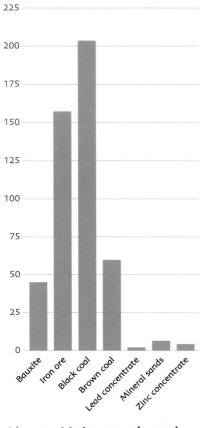

Million tonnes

Above. **Main metals and other minerals produced.**

5%

22%

73%

■ Service industries ■ Manufacturing industry

□ Agricultural industry

Above. **Types of work. Service industries have the most workers.**

Australia is rich in natural resources, especially minerals. These are mined and treated to make many goods. But few people work in mines or factories.

Metals, fuels and precious stones

The main minerals are iron, bauxite, coal, lead and zinc. Other metals mined include silver, copper, nickel, tin, uranium and gold. Oil and gas are produced in large amounts. Valuable stones such as opals, diamonds, rubies and sapphires are also dug from the ground.

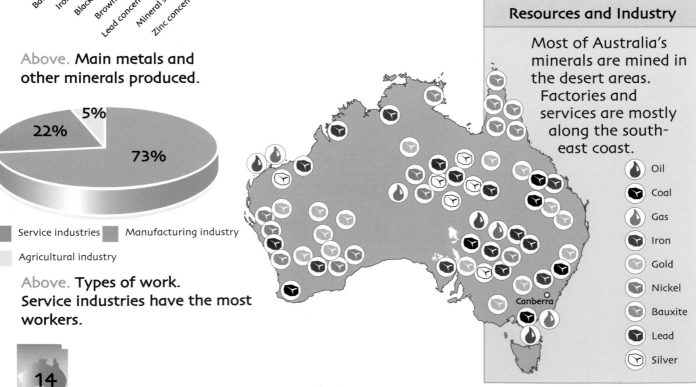

Resources and Industry

Most of Australia's minerals are mined in the desert areas. Factories and services are mostly along the south-east coast.

Oil
Coal
Gas
Iron
Gold
Nickel
Bauxite
Lead
Silver

Canberra

Major industries

Australia is one of the world's largest producers of meat, dairy products and animal feed. Other industries include chemicals, plastics, electronics, paper and steel. Factories make machinery, vehicles and home appliances such as cookers.

Most of Australia's workers are in the service industry. They include teachers and people working in banks, post offices, shops, restaurants, hotels and government offices.

Energy Production

Australia has a lot of coal, oil and natural gas. These are used as fuels.

Most of the country's electricity is produced by coal-fired power stations. Australia's reserves of coal make electricity quite cheap. In some homes in the Outback, people use solar power as a source of energy.

Right. **At this mine in Western Australia, huge machines scrape iron ore from the rocks.**

Web Search ▶▶

▶ www.isr.gov.au
www.dewrsb.gov.au
Government departments for industry and employment.

▶ www.australianmining.com.au/
www.nrm.qld.gov.au/mines/
All about mining and energy resources in Western Australia and Queensland.

▶ www.abs.gov.au
Australian government facts and figures about people, education, housing, work and different types of industries.

Transport

In Australia, distances between places can be so great that a good transport system is essential. Road travel is the most popular, but railways and airlines are used a lot by people and businesses.

Roads and railways

There are nearly one million kilometres of roads, connecting all of the major cities. Cars, buses and coaches carry people. Large trucks, called road trains, pull heavy cargoes across the Outback. There are over 11 million registered motor vehicles in Australia.

The Trans-Australian Railway takes goods from factories and mines to seaports. Australia's trains also carry some 600 million passengers a year. The Indian-Pacific Railway, a luxury train, takes tourists across the whole country, from Sydney to Perth. There are no trains in Tasmania.

In the City

In cities, people use buses, trains and underground trains. They also ride bicycles. Melbourne and Adelaide have electric trams that run on the streets. In Sydney, a monorail runs through the city. Some people travel to work or school by taking a hydrofoil or ferry across the harbour.

Below. **Road trains can pull lots of trailers across the vast Outback.**

Boats and planes

Australia's main ports include Sydney, Melbourne and Brisbane. They handle passenger and cargo ships. There are more than 400 airports, but most handle only internal flights. Sydney Airport is the busiest international airport.

Above. **This Boeing 747 belongs to Qantas, Australia's international airline.**

'000	0	100	200	300	400	500	4.5m	5m
Train								
Bus								
Tram/ferry								
Taxi								
Car (as driver)								
Car (as passenger)								
Motor bike/scooter								
Bicycle								
Walking								

Above. **The different ways Australians travel to work.**

Railways 33,819km (2,540 electrified)

Highways (rough surface) 559,669km

Highways (tarmacked) 353,331km

Waterways 8,668km

Above. **The lengths of Australia's railways, roads and waterways.**

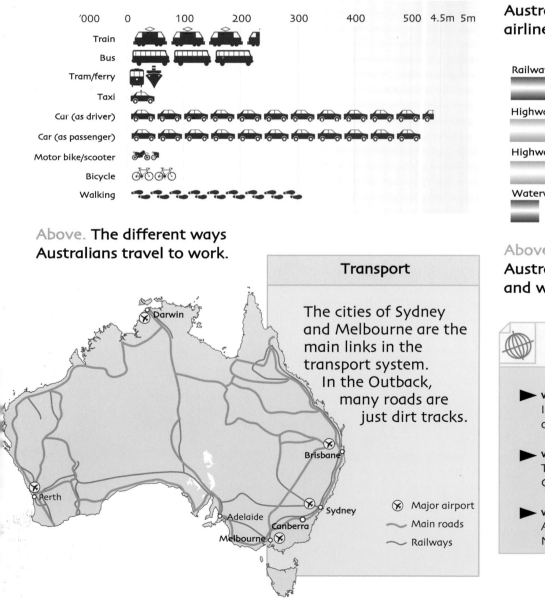

Transport

The cities of Sydney and Melbourne are the main links in the transport system. In the Outback, many roads are just dirt tracks.

Darwin
Brisbane
Perth
Adelaide
Sydney
Canberra
Melbourne

⊗ Major airport
∼ Main roads
∼ Railways

Web Search ▶▶

▶ www.dotrs.gov.au
Information about transport on land, on water and by air.

▶ www.atcouncil.gov.au
The Australian Transport Council.

▶ www.rta.nsw.gov.au
About roads and traffic in New South Wales.

Education

The Schools of the Air programme was set up in 1950. Students tune in to a two-way radio to talk to a teacher far away. The service has now been improved with new telephone and Internet technology.

For Australians, the school year starts in January or early February and ends in December. In the Outback, where there are no towns, Schools of the Air provides a way for children to learn.

School age and the school day

Children go to school from age six to age 15 or 16. Primary and secondary education are free, although some children go to private, fee-paying schools. Classes start at 9 a.m. and end around 3.30 p.m. After school, children go home to study or practise sports.

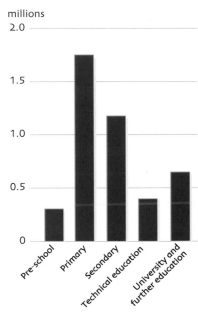

Above. **The number of pupils being taught.**

Left. **These university students in Melbourne are studying the geography of Australia.**

School and beyond

Children start primary school at the age of six. After Year 6 or 7, they enter secondary school, where they stay until Year 10. Children study science, Australian history, mathematics, English, music and art. When they are 15 or 16, students can leave school and go to work, or go to a college that will train them for a job. After this they can go on to study at a university.

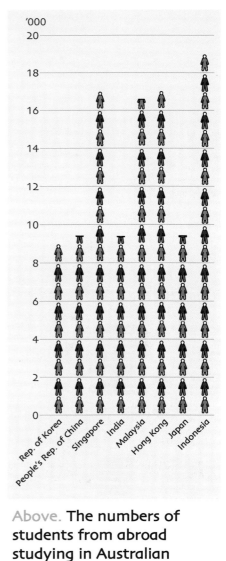

Above. **The numbers of students from abroad studying in Australian universities and colleges.**

Above. **A group of primary school-children take a break on an outing to a museum.**

Web Search ▶▶

▶ www.detya.gov.au
Commonwealth Department of Education, Training and Youth Affairs.

▶ www.eddept.wa.edu.au
www.dete.sa.gov.au/
Departments of Education for Western and South Australia.

Sport and Leisure

The warm climate allows Australians to take part in a wide variety of outdoor sports. More than a third of the population plays organized sports.

Sports and pastimes

Children play many games including netball, cricket, tennis, football, rugby league, rugby union, Australian Rules football and hockey. On the coast, surfing, swimming, scuba-diving, surfboat racing, sailing and fishing are popular. Elsewhere, pastimes include hiking, cycling, horseriding, tennis, badminton, polo and golf. Netball is the most popular sport among women.

Australian Rules Football

'Aussie Rules' is a rough and active game. It was first played in 1858. In September each year, more than 100,000 people gather to watch the Aussie Rules Grand Final game held in Melbourne.

Right. **Sailing in Whitsunday Passage, near the Great Barrier Reef.**

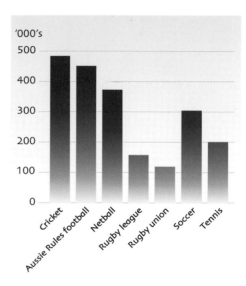

Above. **Australian Rules football is a mix of soccer and rugby. It is a fast and furious game.**

Right. **Membership of different sports clubs.**

Olympic spirit

In 2000, Sydney hosted the 27th Summer Olympic Games. Stadium Australia was built in the city to hold the athletics events. Australians were proud to be chosen to host the Olympics in such a special year, and to be recognized for their sporting tradition.

Web Search ▶▶

▶ www.australia.com/
Australian Tourist Board site.

▶ www.acb.com.au/
Australian Cricket Board site.

▶ www.afl.com.au/
Australian Rules football site.

Daily Life and Religion

In Australia, a family normally wakes up at around 7 a.m. The working day is usually from 9 a.m. to 5 p.m.

Healthy living outdoors

Children spend their free time playing sports or going to the Boy Scouts or Girl Guides. With their parents, they may go to the beach or visit a national park or shopping centre. In fine weather, Australians often have a 'barbie' (barbecue) outdoors where meat or seafood is grilled over hot charcoal.

Australia has its own army, navy and air force, which people can join when they are 17. There is a public healthcare system, paid for by the taxes that all workers pay. Children and the elderly get free healthcare.

The Royal Flying Doctor Service

In the Outback, the doctor's surgery may be hundreds of kilometres away. In an emergency, the Royal Flying Doctor Service (RFDS) sends medical staff out in small planes. Patients are treated on the spot or flown to the nearest hospital.

Below. **Families relaxing on the beach in Perth.**

Below. **Numbers of cars, telephones and TVs for every 1,000 people in the population.**

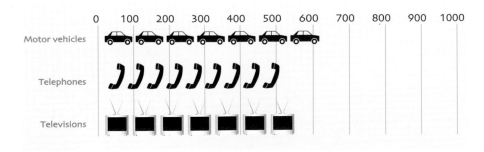

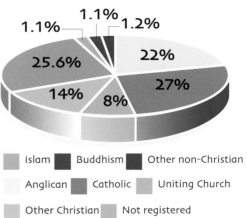

1.1%   1.1%   1.2%
25.6%   22%
14%   27%
8%

Above. **The percentage of Australians following each main religion.**

🌐 **Web Search ▶▶**

▶ **www.aihw.gov.au**
About health and welfare in Australia.

▶ **www.catholic.org.au**
The Catholic Church in Australia.

▶ **www.defence.gov.au**
The Department of Defence.

Above. **Aboriginal rock art about Dreamtime – their story of Creation.**

Religion

Most people in Australia are Christians, but Islam, Buddhism and Judaism are also practised. Aborigines keep up their traditional beliefs of 'Dreamtime' and the spirit world.

Arts and Media

The mix of peoples in Australia has brought an amazing choice of magazines, radio stations and television channels.

Music, dance and art

The government helps to pay for many arts events. All main cities have art museums, orchestras, opera and theatre. The Aboriginal people have a lively artistic culture. At corroborees, they gather to dance and play music. Aboriginal paintings depict people, animals and mythical creatures on bark, cave walls or wood.

Australia's Most Popular Song

The most popular traditional song of Australia is called 'Waltzing Matilda.' It was written in 1895.

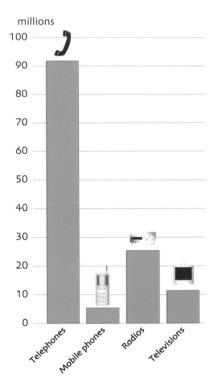

Above. **Total number of electronic goods.**

Left. **The Sydney Opera House, completed in 1973, is a famous landmark.**

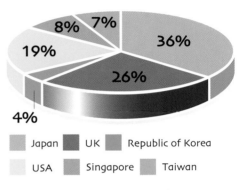
8% 7%
19% 36%
26%
4%

Japan | UK | Republic of Korea
USA | Singapore | Taiwan

Above. **Shoppers are entertained by dancers** at an arcade in Cairns, Queensland.

Above. **Where Australia's tourists come from.**

The media, broadcasting and tourism

More than 1,200 magazines and newspapers are published in Australia. The *Australian* is the country's only national daily newspaper.

The government runs the Australian Broadcasting Corporation (ABC), which provides radio and television without commercials. There is also a number of commercial radio and television stations.

Over four million people visit Australia each year. They relax on beaches, visit historical sites, trek through the rainforest and snorkel along the Great Barrier Reef.

Web Search ▶▶

▶ www.abc.net.au
The Australian Broadcasting Corporation.

▶ www.smh.com.au
The Sydney *Morning Herald* newspaper.

▶ www.ozco.gov.au
The Australian Council for the Arts.

▶ www.artsinfo.net.au
A website with links to dance, film, theatre and museum sites.

Government

Australia is a democracy based on the British system of government. Australia was once a British colony but became an independent nation in 1901.

Voting system

The head of state is Queen Elizabeth II. She does not rule Australia, but appoints a governor-general to represent her. Members of parliament are elected by people aged 18 or over. In Australia, people who can vote must do so and are fined if they do not.

Below. **The Australian parliament meets in this building in Canberra.**

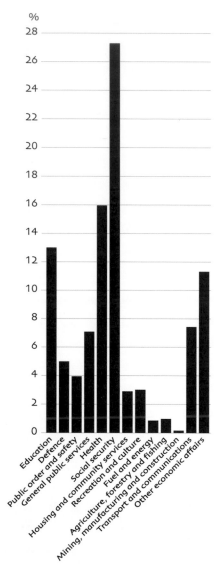

%
28
26
24
22
20
18
16
14
12
10
8
6
4
2
0

Education
Defence
Public order and safety
General public services
Health
Social security
Housing and community services
Recreation and culture
Fuel and energy
Agriculture, forestry and fishing
Mining, manufacturing and construction
Transport and communications
Other economic affairs

Above. **What the government spends on different services and industries.**

26

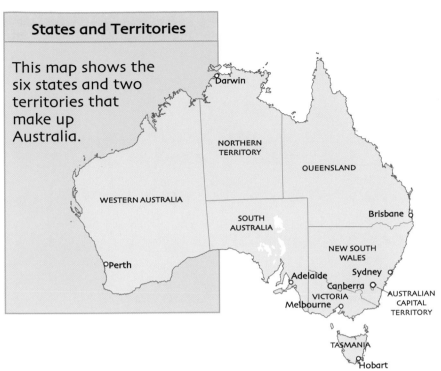

States and Territories

This map shows the six states and two territories that make up Australia.

Darwin

NORTHERN TERRITORY

QUEENSLAND

WESTERN AUSTRALIA

SOUTH AUSTRALIA

Brisbane

Perth

NEW SOUTH WALES

Adelaide

Sydney

Canberra

VICTORIA

AUSTRALIAN CAPITAL TERRITORY

Melbourne

TASMANIA

Hobart

Who Governs What?

The government is in charge of defence, income taxes and immigration policy.

The state and territorial governments are in charge of education, transport, healthcare and the police. Local councils are in charge of housing, roads and waste disposal.

The prime minister

The House of Representatives makes the laws, which are then voted on by the Senate. Members of the House and Senate belong to political parties. The leader of the biggest party becomes the prime minister. He or she chooses members of parliament to make up the Cabinet, which helps the prime minister make decisions. States and territories have their own governments.

DATABASE

How parliament is organized

The House of Representatives has 148 seats. Representatives are elected for up to three years. The Senate has 76 seats. Senators sit for 6 years. Each state and territory elects its own members of parliament.

Web Search ▶▶

► www.australia.gov.au/
The Australian government's website.

► www.aph.gov.au
The Australian parliament's website.

► www.pm.gov.au
The Australian prime minister's official website.

Place in the World

Australia plays a major part in the politics and economics of South-east Asia because of its size and location.

Exports and imports

Australia earns a lot of money from its exports, most of which go to Japan. Among the main exports are farm products (including wheat and wool), minerals and other raw materials, and manufactured goods. Coal and cotton are exported, too. Tourism brings in a lot of money. Australia's main imports are cars and computers, and these come from the European Union (EU), the United States (USA) and Japan.

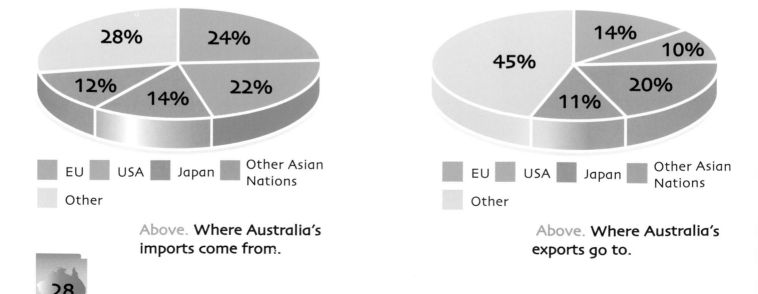

28% 24% 12% 14% 22%

EU   USA   Japan   Other Asian Nations

Other

Above. **Where Australia's imports come from.**

14% 10% 45% 20% 11%

EU   USA   Japan   Other Asian Nations

Other

Above. **Where Australia's exports go to.**

28

Above. **The Great Barrier Reef is more than 2,200km long and is home to more than 10,000 different species.**

Web Search ▶▶

▶ **www.dfat.gov.au**
Department of Foreign Affairs and Trade.

▶ **www.ausaid.gov.au**
Australia's overseas aid plans.

▶ **www.crystalinks.com/australia history.html**
The story of Australia.

Climate Change

Australians are very worried about the effect global warming is having on their country. The Australian government has given almost A$1 billion to reduce 'greenhouse gas' emissions. It wants to protect Queensland's Great Barrier Reef.

Below. **Major exports, in billions of Australian dollars.**

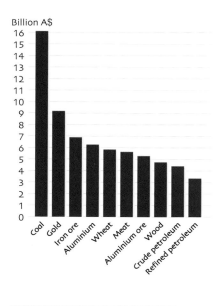

Billion A$

Coal, Gold, Iron ore, Aluminium, Wheat, Meat, Aluminium ore, Wood, Crude petroleum, Refined petroleum

Looking to the future

The arrival of people from different countries in the last century has helped the Aborigines. They have finally been given the right to claim back land that was taken from them in the past by white settlers.

Today, Australians are thinking about breaking their links with Britain. In a vote held in 1999, more than half voted against doing this, but the debate continues.

29

Area:
7,682,300 sq km

Population size:
19,169,083

Capital city:
Canberra (population 298,000)

Other major cities:
Sydney, Melbourne, Brisbane, Perth, Adelaide, Darwin and Hobart

Longest river:
Murray-Darling River system (3,370 km)

Highest mountain:
Mount Kosciuszko (2,229m)

Flag:
The Australian flag has a background of dark blue, with the Union Jack of the United Kingdom in the upper left corner. Under it is a star called the Commonwealth Star, which represents Australia. The other half of the flag shows the constellation of the Southern Cross, with five stars. The stars are white.

Official language:
English

Currency:
Australian dollar (A$)

Major resources:
Coal, iron, bauxite, lead, zinc, oil, gas, silver, copper, nickel, tin, tungsten, gold, uranium and manganese

Major exports:
Aluminium, beef, coal, iron ore, bauxite, wheat, wool, machinery and vehicles

National holidays and major events:
New Year's Day (1 January)
Australia Day (26 January)
Regatta Day, Tasmania (February)
Commonwealth Day (March)
Good Friday, Easter Saturday, Easter Day and Easter Monday (March or April)
ANZAC Day (25 April)
May Day (first Monday in May)
Mothers' Day (May)
Queen's Official Birthday (June)
Fathers' Day (September)
Melbourne Cup Day (November)
Christmas Day (25 December)
Boxing Day (26 December)
Proclamation Day (26 December)

Religions:
Christianity (Roman Catholicism, Anglican, Uniting Church of Australia and others), Islam, Buddhism, Judaism, Hinduism, Sikhism, Baha'i, Aboriginal traditional beliefs, Chinese traditional beliefs

Key Words

ABORIGINAL
Related to the Aborigines, the native peoples of Australia.

BAUXITE
Rock containing aluminium.

CLIMATE
The average weather conditions experienced in one area over a period of time.

COLONY
An area of land that is taken over, settled and ruled by another country.

ECONOMICS
The study of business, money, industry and resources.

EQUATOR
An imaginary line around the middle of the globe. It divides the northern and southern hemispheres.

EXPORTS
The goods and services a country sells to other countries.

DEMOCRACY
A system of government in which people freely vote for representatives for a fixed length of time.

DROUGHT
Long periods without rain.

GOVERNMENT
The organization that sets and enforces laws for a nation.

GRAZING
Feeding on grass and shrubs in fields and open areas.

IMMIGRATION
When people come from one country to live in another.

IMPORTS
The goods and services a country buys from other countries.

LIVESTOCK
Animals that are raised on a farm for their meat, milk, wool and skins.

MANUFACTURED
Products made from raw materials using machinery.

POPULATION
The number of people who live in a certain area.

RESOURCES
A country's supplies of energy, natural materials and minerals.

SERVICE INDUSTRIES
Industries which provide a service to people rather than make products.

SUBURBS
Areas of housing surrounding city and town centres.

Index